Balancing Act

Felicia Black

Presentation by *BookLeaf Publishing*

Web: www.bookleafpub.com

E-mail: info@bookleafpub.com

ISBN: 978-93-5761-001-8

First edition 2022

Mixed Up

I don't know
What to believe anymore.
Hypocrites
Critics
And finicky old men
All shake their heads
And whisper behind dusty, ivory curtains
So my morals are mixed up
And my heart's lost for words.
My conscience can barely decide
Whether it's coming or going.
I'm starting to wonder
If they believe for the right reasons
Or rather,
For the security of that Better Place.
Maybe they'll be reincarnated as an old potato,
or a dime
Lost beneath the suffocating barriers
Of gaudy wine colored corduroy
Sofa cushions.

I Am From

I am from a crowd of slaves
    Beaten,
        Broken,
            And practically dead now.

From a place where dreams won't become
realities
And rewards never follow work, not even on
birthdays.

I am from late night telephone calls
    [whispers of best friends and ex-lovers]

   And from too many harmful habits
with scanty self-esteem.

I am from seduction
               blackened and sick
charred pieces of what someone called ♡love♡

From broken heart s l i c e s
Bandaged with sutures, staples, & glitter glue

And from O's instead of exes
because they aren't as hard on my eyes.

I am from everything that has ever
been wrong with us

From parasitic barbs that feed you without limit
& bury themselves inside your shell

And from a loaded gun
          filled with rock-salt,
                    nails,
                    & b-r-o-k-e-n glass.

I'm from lonely nights when my companion was
a razor
          & crimson cut across my sheets.

From denial and withdrawal:
                    losing all sensation.

And from too much Tylenol
with a hopeful side effect of DEATH.

Most days, I wish I was from the day before
yesterday.

I already know how that day ends.

Some Haiku - ten views.

ONE
how do you function?
breathing. sharp in and sharp out.
this is just starting.

TWO
insecurities.
is it my shirt or do you
judge me by my size?

THREE
all those lies wash down
my fears. now all i have left
to digest is me.

FOUR
let the water run
to drown the sound while you make
your insides spill out.

FIVE
empty inside but
at least she's pretty. it's beau-
ty at her blackest.

SIX
do you want to be
worthless? you're acting all nine-
ty-nine cents again.

SEVEN
you know, i'm not the
carefullest of girls. of course.
this is all your fault.

EIGHT
is it black and white?
in the scheme of things, what is
one more sleepless night?

NINE
times like these make me
think the ugliest thoughts a
pretty girl could think.

TEN
size zero and it
hurts — no one will tell her she's
god damn beautiful.

Rituals

Eyes shut, but I can't sleep.
The door stumbles open
As stars begin to dot the sky.
I begin to count. One. Two.
Three.
How much longer?
Thirty-five. Thirty-six.
They're beautiful really, so pretty.

I cough, sputter,
Curse the foul fumes
That now fill my lungs
And seep into my blood.
Breathe out.
Remember.
Remember to breathe.
Of course I remember.
Eighty-three. Eighty-four.
How could I forget?

This feeling, sensation,
Tingling in my fingertips,
Butterflies in my stomach,
Is my despair.
Ninety-nine. One-hundred.

Wide-eyed arcs of
Brilliant white hot light
Tear voraciously through
The pin-holed indigo canvas.
The windowed view starts to ease
The swollen stress
Of these depraved acts.
And me, their sole proprietor.

This is full-bodied betrayal
Coming to a head.

Black Widow

Fear.
Black,
But vivid crimson.
Appalling.
Shocking.
Spinning.
Provoking.
Overwhelming and yet
SO
tiny.

Eight legs.
High places.
Camouflaged.
Enclosed spaces.

Fear.
False
Evidence
Appearing
Real.

Emphasizing
Negatives.
Overlooking

Positives.
Creating some
Jumbled
And Broken
Snare.

Fear.
Of what?
Backbiting
Arachnids,
Dare I say,
Parents.?
Spouses.?
Lethal Fangs
Hover.
Abusive.
Unhealthy.
Lying low until
The ambush.
Deadly.

Toxin
Introduces
Violent illustrations
of
Electric hallucinations.
Ultra violet
Fright.
Suggests.

Supports.
Shows
No form of
Cover.
Simply,
Fear.

Now,
You express,
Fear.
Introduces itself
as
Difficult.
To control.
You say,
Lies.
Untruths.
Fear.
can be
Tamed.
And conclude
that
Fear.
is a Hoax.

Well,
Imagine.
Your best friend
Is fading.

Your daddy,
Your hero.
Superman.
He's dying.

Suppose,
Dear reader,
This happened
To
You.

Fear.
Of losing
A father.
A friend.

Fear.
That part of
You
Will die
With him.

Fear.
With
No one
To stand
Behind you.
Beside you.
Between you

(and the widow).
To protect you
From the venom
Of the raging mother.

Fear.
Black,
But so vivid.
Crawling
And pulsing,
Fixed
Inside me.

Control it.
I dare you.

Closing Scene

The heart monitor screams.
Silence.

Remote walls encase this picture.
Toxic signs staining sanitized surfaces.
Needles and tubes sticking in and sucking out.
He rests on a plastic mattress
Unfit for a spirit so free.
Heavy limbs and a chest with no rhythm.
He's shrunken and faded.
Oh, he is so [c]old.

Sixty-seven acts.
Over two-million scenes.
Importance and integrity in each stage.
His stubborn smile present through the last
breath.
What a man.

Applause.
Remarkable theatrics.
And here,
The guise of a genuine dead man.
What a show.

Crowds clear.
Curtains fade.
The set is taken apart.
Rearranged.
Given away.
Trashed entirely by the mother
And her new lover.

Dramas
Comedies
And tragedies
Open and end.
This performance is forgotten
In the frantic rush of life.

Don't forget.
I'm still standing
There.
Where you won't find me.
Petrified.
Upstage.

End final act
Of Daddy's existence.

City, Come Winter

The sea of people
clad in coats and scarves
and the occasional mini skirt
that pushes, shoves,
and crowds the sidewalk
making it impossible to get anywhere
as quickly as you would like to

Stream of yellow taxi cabs,
weaving through the cars
a cacophony of horns

Billboards,
advertising what you would never buy
if you really stopped to think,
headache-inducing lights, colors, noise
and gaudy holiday decoration

The occasional corner saxophonist
or a Peruvian gentleman,
clutching his panpipes
scattered amidst the street vendors
and the million and one Starbucks

Even in the dark
there is artificial brightness
and a twist of smoke
as yet another cigarette falls

to the ground
to be twisted
into the pavement
by a stiletto heeled boot

Go

Let it go.
Mourn what you had
hoped for.
Let the trees
breathe you.
Let the sun
see you.
Let the seasons
heal you.
Let it stop feeling
like failing
And begin to feel

like freedom.

24.7.365

If days were seconds
This would all be over before Saturday morning
cartoons.

We'd be found out,
		tied up,
		and tired enough,
Underneath your blankets
With our fingers in our ears
Our eyes wrinkled,
			stiff,
	and swollen shut.

Or maybe in the shadowy basement
Of a long forgotten century home
Past the doors that won't close
(warped from 3 months of the sun's tyranny)
And behind the doors that were never opened
(bound by sweat and human hair)

It doesn't matter who finds us.
Because we would become
Silhouettes,
	Phantoms,
		Vapor.

Or a combination of the three.

With our palms and toes lashed together,
With telephone wires
And sutured with Peanuts postage stamps.
We'd slow dance forever.
                "You're changing me,"
                                I'd say.

You laugh,
And look back at me,
I can see it now.

If days were seconds,
This year would be ours.

Pitch

The hot ebony and ivory mingle
Intertwined
Chasing and complementing each other
Softly
And then loudly, like we do.

We breathe these notes together
Burning between jealous bars
Under
And around each other
Harmonizing
Humming melodies made for symphonies.

Slowly, then all at once, our tune pours
Into each beat
Beautiful bursts arcing across impossible keys
Lingering
In the embrace of each savory solo.

Staccato breaths
Playing
Infinite across our night
And our tired fingers
Tremble
At the piercing rests and insatiable crescendos.

"I love you," spills out
With perfect vibrato
And a touch of falsetto
Blazing
Brighter than the white hot music of our
moonlight.

Brilliant blacks and brights play on
Cascading chords pleasing
Teasing
Beckoning
The unrequited passion in our not-so-silent sky.

"Love me, just a little louder now"
And, repeat.

gre;Enly

my ♡love♡
 i think we have
groWN
treeLy;Your
limbsagainstmy
limbs, my face all
nTAgleNadGtdeLlgEtedDge
in your [rustling
Growing greenlYbreathingbranches];
you are at the

     c

     e

     n

     t

     e

     r

of all this (it is YOUR rooot)s—
from here, we are upsidedownways(in
each other twining)
&&;up to the wide blue sky.

Bottom to Top

You lay
On my kitchen floor
With no shirt on
Your fevered cheek
Resting for a moment
Against the cool
Linoleum
It was white
With squares
The same bright blue
As your eyes
And I knew
That no matter
What I did
I could never lift you
Up off that floor
So I turned the house
Upside down
And you fell onto the ceiling
Where you belong

The Doctor Game

Can't quite explain these words
in just the right way
to make you
understand
this ♡heart♡.
I know all it is
is a pound of flesh.
A bloody, beating, pound.
But, do you know
how it hurts?
I'm not even sure I do.
But it does baby.
[Oh, it does.]
Not saying yours doesn't.
We're all these broken ♡hearts♡
right now.
In so many pieces.
But inside all the pieces
are just more
whole
little
you's
with every broken ♡heart♡ piece.

Whisper

Whisper loudly again why you hate me
Pierce my sweet peace with false words and
sharp looks
Drain fuel from my heart
Bleed life from my fingers
Destroy me to build your ego.
Brick after brick climb higher
But be wary stranger, for I have not died
The deafening crash of your insecurities could
awaken the devil.

Fold

One by one the years submit
And I turn my head,
Too ashamed to watch.
Carefully I fold them,
Days and months and weeks,
Bending corner to corner
In straight and permanent lines
Creased and smooth.
Curled with knees to chin
I divide life among tiny potted greenery
Arranging them across this dusty
Window ledge in tightly forced rows.
I write words across these pages
That are tucked away, dismissed.
Even when I see you now,
Or think it may be your familiar silhouette
In passing traffic, my slender fingers
Remember how to fold.

With You

I imagined walking away would be the hardest.
But it's not.
It's staying gone.
Letting my heart hurt instead of seeking you to
treat the wound.
Teaching my fingertips to settle for something
else when they instinctively reach for you.
It's crying myself to sleep.
Staying up all night.
Choosing loneliness over you again and again.
It's realizing it's better to be sad on occasion
now
Than feel constant heartache with you.

The Crimes We Commit

It was a Sunday.
Glory had failed and he was prepared for
punishment & sickness & suffering.
He said it was worth it, for me.

He was inspiring, crucial to this story,
even donated his courage.
Now he has given into the war;
the armies assembled around him,
burning eyes following.
He was prepared to raze nations,
I could tell.

He could be invincible,
harden his heart to everyone
until only I could feel it beat.
He thought he had nothing to show.
No blood. No guts.
No scars.

I held sharp objects,
designing wounds to pour salt into.
Punishing the thought of trying again.
He had reasons to bleed and mine were
so different; mine always lacked sense.

He tried saving me,
cutting me out of the world in a heart-shaped
Valentine.
I didn't deserve that form,
thinking like I do.

I could never let go
of what I accidentally discovered.
I panicked —
I didn't have an answer.
And I could never
repay that debt.

I would lie awake for him.
Smell his hair in my thoughts.
Tear into his soul in my dreams,
and then realize
I was wrong.

I wouldn't let him love me
in the best ways he could.
So instead, I built a wall
when I should've made a window.
It was all I had to give.

Cups

So she takes care of them. Days in and days out.
Filling cups that aren't hers. And she never says
it out loud — how she so badly wants to be
taken care of.

And that makes her feel selfish and weak.
Because she was raised to handle life on her own
and never depend on others. To fill everyone's
cup, even if hers ran dry. And to be sure they
were all taken care of.

But every once in a while her empty cup tips and
tumbles, and the tiredness overtakes her. She is
overcome with loneliness. And a hefty need to
be taken care of.

Safe

Little One,

I never forgot you.

I see you -
Your sadness and sorrow.
Your broken, weary soul.

Thank you.
For protecting us.
For hiding the memories.
For building the walls.

You did the best with what you knew.

I hear you.
Your scared heart screaming.
Your panic on this path to healing.

Thank you.
For being the one we could count on.
For acting tough and unaffected.
For keeping us safe for so long.

But you're safe now.
You can rest.
You can let it all go.

I'm showing up for us now.

Make Room

Identify the anger
Pull apart the shame
Remove the isolation
Keep the hurt at bay
Feel through the frustration
Let sadness run its course
Let out all the outrage
And make room for the grief.

Heal.

Heal.
Because your soul is tired.
Because your gifts aren't meant to be hidden.
Because your productivity doesn't define your purpose.
Because your imperfections don't decide your worth.
Because your journey is to show up in all the ways they didn't.
Because it's all connected.
Heal.
Because the world deserves the whole you.

9 789357 610018